THE BOOK OF
PITCH
EXPLORATION

Can Your Voice Do This?

G-5276

THE BOOK OF

PITCH EXPLORATION

Can Your Voice Do This?

John M. Feierabend

GIA PUBLICATIONS, INC. · CHICAGO

Created by
John M. Feierabend
First Steps in Music, LLC

www.giamusic.com/feierabend

Artwork: Tim Phelps
Editor: Lillie Feierabend
Layout: Nina Fox

Copyright © 2003
GIA Publications, Inc.
7404 S. Mason Avenue
Chicago, IL 60638

Printed in the
United States of America.
ISBN 1-57999-265-X

Table of Contents

Introduction

This book contains activities that help children discover the sounds they can make with their voices. Not only are they wonderfully fun, but they serve as excellent vocal warm-ups for singing.

Just as an athlete warms up various muscles before he or she competes, singers warm up their vocal muscles in order to be able to sing with flexibility, especially in the higher range.

The stories in this book invite vocal participation. The poems are spoken with extreme inflection, and children simply love the vocal sliding activities.

The Pitch Exploration activities are full of wonder, magic, and make-believe. Not only are they enjoyable, they are good for you!

So, come on and explore the sounds your voice can make. You will have a great time while developing your vocal muscles!

John M. Feierabend

IDEAS

Back Shapes

Students should work in groups of two. Have one student "draw" on the back of his or her partner. Instruct the student whose back is being drawn on to make a sound with his or her voice that matches the shape of the drawing they are feeling. Switch roles.

Bounce, Aim and Shoot

Lead the class in the following chant:

"Bounce, bounce, bounce, bounce, aim, and shoot!"

Each time the students say "bounce," they should pretend to bounce a basketball one time on the ground. When the students say "aim," they should pause and pretend to hold their basketballs in a shooting position. Finally, when they students say "shoot," which they should sustain as a descending glissando, they should pretend to throw the ball toward the basket and then slowly lower their arms.

After the class has tried this exercise as a group, instruct individuals to "bounce, aim, and shoot" on their own.

Elevator Operator Shapes

Tell your students to pretend that they are elevator operators in a 12-floor building. As a class, you will make the elevator go up and down to pick up people on different floors. To show that the elevator is going up, students should place their arms above their heads and make an ascending glissando sound with their voices. To show that the elevator is going down, students should lower their arms and make a descending glissando sound. Because making descending sounds ensures that the head voice is engaged, be sure to start on the 12th floor.

Later, arrange the students in a single-file line and have them come forward, one by one, to operate the elevator individually. Start the first student on the 12th floor and then have each subsequent student begin on the floor where the previous student ended.

Find Your Family

Think of a few animals whose sounds would work well for pitch exploration.

Cow - moo
Cat - meow
Whale - mmmm
Horse - neeeee
Crow - caw
Etc…

Once you have a few animals in mind (four or five for a class of 20 should suffice), assign an animal to each student in the class. Ask students to find the others in their animal "family" by making their animal's sound. Once all the students have found their families, ask each family to make its sound one more time for the class.

Find Your Partner

Create a set of glissandi flashcards (draw a line on an index card to represent the shape of a vocal glissando). Make sure that there are two of each card, then distribute the cards to your students. Challenge students to find their card's mate by making the sound that they think their flashcard makes.

If two students think that their sounds are the same, they may show each other their cards. If the cards match, they may sit down. If they do not match, they must continue to search.

Continue the game until all are sitting.

Helium Balloon

Raise and lower a helium balloon by pulling its string through your thumb and forefinger. As your students watch the balloon move up and down, instruct them to make glissando sounds to match the balloon's movement.

Parachute Game

Have your students hold onto the sides of a sheet or small parachute. Instruct the students to lift the sheet above their heads and to slowly let it flow down. Have the students follow the motion of the sheet with their voices.

Pass the Owl

Seat your students in a circle. Pretend to hold an owl, then raise and lower it in the air. As you lower the owl, lead the students in making a falling vocal glissando on "Whooooo." Each person should raise and lower the owl two times, then pass it to their neighbor. Continue passing the owl until all have had a turn. Strive for a beautiful sustained sound.

Yarn Shapes (Floor Yarn)

Divide students into small groups, and give each group a long piece of yarn. Have an individual in each group create a shape with the yarn on the floor (or on a feltboard). The one who made the shape should point to the yarn and follow it from one end to the other while the others in his or her group perform sliding sounds with their voices to match the shape of the yarn. Repeat until all have had a turn to create a yarn shape.

Flashlight

Find a flashlight with a strong, focused beam. Shine the flashlight on a wall and slowly move the beam up and down and in various shapes. Have the whole class make sliding sounds with their voices to reflect the way the beam is moving.

Later, have individuals take turns holding the flashlight.

Flying Puppets

Find or make a puppet of an animal that flies (bird, butterfly, ghost, etc.). Move the puppet in various directions and have students create vocal glissandi as they follow the puppet's movement. Later, allow individuals to put on the puppet and lead the class.

Pattern Memory

Demonstrate four different vocal glissando sounds and assign a hand signal to represent each sound. Once your students have memorized the hand signals, encourage them to make the appropriate sound when you show the signal. Gradually increase the speed.

Pipe Cleaners

Make several bends in a pipe cleaner and hold it in front of the class. With one finger, trace the outline of the pipe cleaner as you instruct your students to make vocal sliding sounds to match the rise and fall of the pipe cleaner shape.

Later, try this exercise in small groups with students leading their classmates. Continue until everyone has had a chance to be the leader for their group.

Pitch Conducting

Use a baton to "conduct" your students in making vocal glissandi. Move your hand down, up, and around as students use their voices to match the direction of the baton.

Later, have individuals take turns "conducting" the class.

Ribbon on a Stick

Attach a long piece of ribbon (about 10 feet) to a stick. Wave the stick so that the ribbon creates a flowing pattern in the air. Have your students match the shapes made by the ribbon by vocally sliding their voices.

Later, invite individuals to lead the class.

Roller Coaster

Find a picture of a roller coaster track or draw one on a blackboard. Have the students slide with their voices as you trace the course of the roller coaster.

Later try reversing the activity. Invite individual students to make vocal sliding sounds while the rest of the class draws what they hear.

Rubber Bands

Pull on a rubber band while your students slide their voices (Silly Putty will also work). Because making descending sounds ensures that the head voice is engaged, be sure to start with downward pulls before you start to vary directions.

Later, invite individuals to lead the group.

Squirt Gun

Squirt water from a squirt gun and tell your students to make glissando sounds to match the shape of the spray. Aim the squirt gun in different directions to achieve different vocal glissandi sounds.

Sirens

Divide your students into three groups. One group will be the siren for a police car, one group will be the siren for an ambulance, and one group will be the siren for a fire truck. Suggest various situations and have the appropriate group respond with their siren sound.

Example:
A burglar! (police)
Cat stuck in a tree (fire truck)
Someone fainted (ambulance)
Etc.

Instrumental Glissandi

Glissando sounds can be made on various instruments, such as:

> Slide Whistle
> Siren Whistle
> Violin (or other string instrument)
> Trombone
> Piano
> Dulcimer
> Kazoo

Invite your students to imitate the sliding instrumental sounds with their voices. Start with descending sounds (which ensures that the head voice is engaged in the sound making), and later add ascending sounds and other sound shapes.

Sound Cards

Create a set of glissandi flashcards (draw a line on an index card to represent the shape of a vocal glissando). Present the flashcards to your students and have them create glissando sounds to match each shape.

Later, allow students to take turns arranging four cards in a row to create a sound composition for the class to perform.

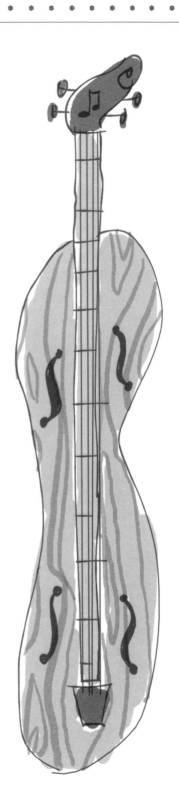

Tape Measure

Pull a tape measure while your students slide their voices. Because making descending sounds ensures that the head voice is engaged, be sure to start with downward pulls before you start to vary directions.

Later, invite individuals to lead the group.

Toss Across

Arrange your students in a circle. Pick one student to hold a beanbag. Tell the student holding the beanbag to pick another student, to say that student's name, and to toss the beanbag to that student. The student who tossed the beanbag should make an ascending and descending vocal glissando that follows the path of the beanbag while it's in the air. He or she should sit as soon as the beanbag is caught.

Continue until all children are sitting.

Toys That Move

The following toys are good for vocal glissando exercises:

Whirligig ("stick helicopter" toy)
Magnetic Wheel ("wheel-o" toy)
Pop-up Puppet
Yo-Yo
Bubbles

Operate each toy, and have your students make sliding sounds with their voices to reflect the way the toy is moving. Later, invite individual students to lead the class.

Wind Game

Lead your students in making "wind" sounds using the vowel sound "oooo." Later, have individual students lead the class.

Play the game of "Hot and Cold." Hide an object and have one student try to find it. If the student gets close to the object, the class should make the wind sound higher and louder. If the student moves away from the object, the class should make the wind sound lower and softer.

Vocal Wave

Arrange your students in a circle, and tell them to turn left or right so they're all facing in one direction. Explain that you're going to start a "wave" like the kind seen in the crowds at major sporting events. Slowly raise and then lower your arms to start the wave. The student standing behind you should start moving his or her arms shortly after you begin, thus leading the third student in line and so on. The raising and lowering motion should continue smoothly around the circle until it arrives back at its starting point. After students are able to perform the wave, have them add an ascending and descending "whoo" sound as their arms move up and then down. Turn and repeat in the opposite direction.

Yawning and Stretching

Stretch and make a yawning sound, then invite your students to imitate the movement and the sound. Create several different yawning sounds. Later, invite individuals to lead the class.

Yoo-Hoo

Assemble your students outside your classroom door and tell them to enter one at a time. Explain that each student must first sing "Yoo-hoo" in a descending fashion before he or she may enter. The sound must be strong enough to reach the opposite end of the room.

Whale Sounds

Play a recording of whale sounds. Ask the students to guess what animal is making those sounds.

Find or make a whale puppet. Use the puppet to "talk whale" to the class (make humming glissando sounds). Later, have two students hold whale puppets and "talk whale" to each other.

Dove variation: "Whoo, Whoo."

Cat variation: "Meow, Meow."

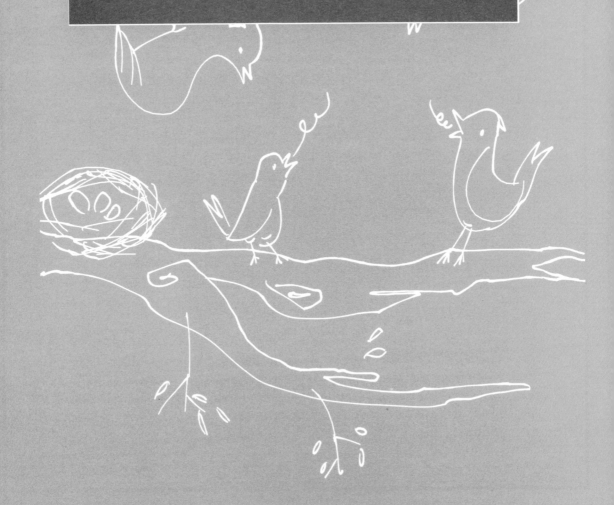

POEMS AND STORIES

Mr. Wiggle and Mr. Waggle

Part 1

This is the story of Mr. Wiggle and Mr. Waggle.
   Hold up the thumb of each hand.
Mr. Wiggle lived in this house,
   Open one hand, fold thumb down, and wrap fingers around the thumb.
And Mr. Waggle lived in this house.
   Open the other hand, fold thumb down, and wrap fingers around the thumb.
One day, Mister Wiggle decided to go visit Mr. Waggle.
So, he opened the gate!
   Open the fingers and make an upward creaking sound.
And he came outside, boop!
   Raise thumb and make a high pitched "boop."
And he closed the gate!
   Close fingers into a fist with thumb still up and make a downward creaking sound.
And he went up the hill and down the hill,
   Raise thumb up high and with great exaggeration have children raise their voices saying, "up the hill" and lower thumbs and voices with "down the hill."

Up the hill and down the hill,
Up the hill and down the hill
Until he got to Mr. Waggle's house.
He knocked on the gate.
Knock, knock, knock, Mr. Waggle!
   Make a knocking motion three times.
Knock, knock, knock.
   Three more knocking motions.
No Mr. Waggle!
So he went
Up the hill and down the hill,
Up the hill and down the hill,
Up the hill and down the hill
Until he got to his house.
He opened the gate!
   Open fingers and make an upward creaking sound.
And he went inside, boop!
   Fold thumb down and make a high pitched "boop."
And he closed the gate!
   Close fingers around thumb and make a downward creaking sound.
And he went to sleep.

Part 2

Well, pretty soon Mr. Waggle decided he would go visit Mr. Wiggle.
So he opened his gate, boop!
   Using other hand, continue story, motions, and sounds as before until "And he went to sleep."

Part 3

Well, pretty soon Mr. Wiggle decided
  to go see Mr. Waggle,
And Mr. Waggle decided to go see
  Mr. Wiggle.
So they opened their gates!
  *Motions and sounds as before with both
  hands.*
And they came outside, boop!
And they closed their gates!
And they went up the hill and down
  the hill,
Up the hill and down the hill,
Up the hill and down the hill
Until all of a sudden they saw each
  other!
And they said, "Hello Mr. Wiggle."
  Wiggle one thumb.
"Hello Mr. Waggle."
  Wiggle the other thumb.
And they talked and they talked and
  they talked,
Until it was time to say "Goodbye."

"Goodbye."
  Wiggle one thumb.
"Goodbye."
  Wiggle the other thumb.
And they went up the hill and down
  the hill.
  *Motion with both hands with extreme
  vocal inflection as before.*
And up the hill and down the hill,
And up the hill and down the hill
Until they got to their houses.
They opened their gates!
  *Open fingers of both hands and make
  an upward creaking sound.*
They went inside, boop!
  *Fold thumbs down and make a high
  pitched "boop."*
They closed their gates!
  *Close fingers around thumbs and make
  a downward creaking sound.*
And they went to sleep.

The End.

Big Pig

"Where are you going, Big Pig, Big
Pig?"
Spoken with a high voice.

"Out in the garden to dig, dig, dig!"
Spoken with a low voice.

"Out in the garden to dig, dig, dig?
Shame on you, Big Pig, Big Pig!"
Spoken with a high voice.

"I'm sorry, ma'am, but I'm only a pig,
And all I can do is dig, dig, dig!"
Spoken with a low voice.

Two Little Puppets

Two little puppets,
One on each hand.
Isn't she pretty?
Isn't he grand?
Her name is Bella.
His name is Beau.
She says, "Good morning."
   High pitched voice.
He says, "Hello."
   Low pitched voice.

*Have your students speak the "Hello" and
"Good morning" parts using the correct
voice placement. Later, have individuals
take turns.*

Whoops, Pardon Me!

I saw you in the orchard,
I saw you in the sea,
I saw you in the bathtub,
Whoops, pardon me!
   *Make an upward vocal slide on
   "Whoops."*

Pussy Cat, Pussy Cat

"Pussy cat, pussy cat where have you been?"

Spoken with a high voice.

"I've been to London to visit the queen."

Spoken with a low voice.

"Pussy cat, pussy cat, what did you there?"

Spoken with a high voice.

"I frightened a little mouse under the chair."

Spoken with a low voice.

The Blue Cockatoo

There's nothing to do,
And I'm feeling so blue,
With all I've been through,
You'd be feeling blue too.
Descending sigh.

I live in this zoo
On the banks of Peru,
With a wonderful view,
But still I'm quite blue. *(sigh)*

You see I am new,
Making this zoo debut,
As a fine cockatoo.
So why am I blue? *(sigh)*

Well, just to review,
I am here in this zoo,
With nothing to do
But sit and be blue. *(sigh)*

Though a cockatoo view
Might be pleasant for you,
If my story you knew,
You might feel blue too. *(sigh)*

I was born in Zulu
Where my white feathers grew.
And I hadn't a clue
Why they soon became blue. *(sigh)*

At first it was new,
Being a blue cockatoo.
No kind of shampoo
Could remove my blue hue. *(sigh)*

But one day as I flew,
A net someone threw.
I wish I knew who
Had found this bird blue. *(sigh)*

So off we soon flew
To a Peruvian zoo.
I bid Zulu adieu
And began feeling blue. *(sigh)*

Now they stand in a queue
To see me be blue.
With each "How do you do?"
I grow even more blue. *(sigh)*

But don't misconstrue,
Being blue in a zoo,
Beats being found on a menu
As blue cockatoo stew. *(sigh)*

— *John M. Feierabend*

I Thought I Heard a Puppy Whine

I thought I heard a puppy whine,
mmm, mmm, mmm
Maybe it was in my mind.
mmm, mmm, mmm
Then again, it might be swine,
mmm, mmm, mmm
No, I'm sure it sounds canine.
mmm, mmm, mmm

Yes, I am quite sure this time,
mmm, mmm, mmm
That I hear a puppy whine,
mmm, mmm, mmm

And I think I see a sign,
mmm, mmm, mmm
That my ears are working fine.
mmm, mmm, mmm

Dad says she's my Valentine,
mmm, mmm, mmm
And her name is Adeline.
mmm, mmm, mmm
See my face begin to shine,
mmm, mmm, mmm
I think she is super fine.
mmm, mmm, mmm

— John M. Feierabend

Cowboy Joe

Cowboy Joe was a bold young man,
He dreamed of rustling cattle, most of
    all.
He wanted to see if the cows would
    come
When he let out his cowboy call.
    yee-haa

He practiced all day from morning to
    night,
And he practiced both summer and
    fall.
He knew some day he'd have his
    chance
To try out his cowboy call.
    yee-haa

Well, finally one day, it was proudly
    annouced
That his ma and pa and all,
Were takin' a trip to his grandfather's
    ranch
Where he could try out his cowboy
    call.
    yee-haa

He jumped for joy and grabbed his
    gear
And he ran back down the hall.
He hopped into the car and was ready
    to go
To let out his cowboy call.
    yee-haa

When he arrived at the ranch he was
    happy to see
That the cows were not in the stall.
He dashed to the field where they
    quietly grazed
And he let out his cowboy call.
    yee-haa

Well they all did come right up to the
    fence
And he sure felt ten feet tall.
"I'm Cowboy Joe. See how the cows
    come
When I let out my cowboy call."
    yee-haa

Now, that was really some day for
    Cowboy Joe
And he sure did have a ball.
Now he's wantin' to try bigger and
    better things;
So he's practicing his elephant call.
    (?)

— *John M. Feierabend*

An Old Woman

Each ghost sound should become more scary.

There was an old woman all skin and
 bone,
She lived on a hillside all alone.
 o-o-o-o-o
She'd go to church one day,
To hear the parson preach and pray.
 o-o-o-o-o

When she got to the churchyard stile,
She thought she'd stop to rest a
 while. *o-o-o-o-o*

When she got to the churchyard
 door,
She thought she'd stop to rest some
 more. *o-o-o-o-o*

And when she got to the church
 within,
She thought she'd stop and rest
 again. *o-o-o-o-o*

She looked up high and then looked
 down,
A ghostly corpse lay on the ground.
 o-o-o-o-o

From eyes and mouth and ears and
 chin,
The worms crawled out and the
 worms crawled in. *o-o-o-o-o*

The woman to the parson said,
"Will I look so when I am dead?"
 o-o-o-o-o

The parson to the woman said,
"Yes, you will look so when you are
 dead." *o-o-o-o-o*

The old woman all skin and bone,
 then said *e-e-e-e-e!*

Andrew Got a Pogo Stick

Children respond to each line saying "boing, boing, boing" in an upward glissando.

Andrew got a pogo stick,
 boing, boing, boing
He could really do that trick,
 boing, boing, boing
Up to fifty, did it quick!
 boing, boing, boing
"How 'bout my arithmetic?"
 boing, boing, boing

Onward still the numbers tick,
 boing, boing, boing
At this task, he ain't no hick,
 boing, boing, boing
Eighty, ninety, this is slick,
 boing, boing, boing
Andrew and his pogo stick,
 boing, boing, boing

–John M. Feierabend

Laugh Like a Loon

Stirring, stirring, 'round in a pot.
Bubbling, bubbling, bubbling hot.
Look at the moon, laugh like a loon.
*Make a downward glissando with your
voice.*
Stir something 'round in the pot.

On a Dark and Stormy Night

*Teach the students the appropriate vocal
sounds to make after each of the following
phrases. Guide the class to ensure they are
making appropriate head voice sounds.*

On a dark and stormy night….

Witches laugh *ha, ha, ha, ha*

Owls hoot *oooooo*

Ghosts swoop *whooosshhh*

Wolves howl *ah-ooooo*

Goblins dance *wheeeeee*

Thunder claps *clap hands together*

People scream *ahhhhhhhhh*

On a dark and stormy night.

The Airplane Ride

*Children respond at the end of the lines
saying either "All right" or "Oh, no" with
rising inflection on the second syllable.*

A man went up in an aiplane,
  All right!
But the plane didn't have an engine,
  Oh, no!
But the man had a parachute,
  All right!
But the parachute wouldn't open,
  Oh, no!
But there was a haystack under him,
  All right!
But there was a pitch fork in the
  haystack.
  Oh, no!
But he missed the pitchfork,
  All right!
But he missed the haystack, too.
  Oh, no!

—John M. Feierabend

The Ice Cream Sundae

Today was a day I did everything
right,
Though my brother annoyed me, I
still didn't fight.
I played nicely all day, didn't argue or
scream,
Now my mom says we'll go for a dish
of ice cream. *mmmm*

I ate all of my breakfast and all of my
lunch,
I picked up my toys (and I have a
bunch),
And since I've been helpful, like part
of a team,
I think I might ask for two scoops of
ice cream. *mmmm*

Two scoops! What a treat! But I
think you'll agree,
It would be hard to imagine one
better than me.
I've done everything right, or so it
would seem,
Maybe Mom will allow me four
scoops of ice cream. *mmmm*

Yes! Today has been special. It's not
every day,
I do everything right, in such a nice
way.
So why not, of course, since I'm
building up steam,
Have some syrup on top of four
scoops of ice cream. *mmmm*

"You've been perfect my dear," That's
what Mom said today,
So I know she won't mind if I have it
my way.
To the syrup, add nuts and also
whipped cream
And a cherry on top of four scoops of
ice cream. *mmmm*

And yet, when I think about wanting
more,
Though it sounds awfully good, I
know what's in store.
I'll eat and I'll eat and I'll run out of
steam,
And I won't feel so good after all that
ice cream. *mmmm*

Since today was a day I did every
thing right,
I will not spoil my record by making a
sight.
I'll ask most politely, though it was
fun to dream,
"May I have one scoop of vanilla ice
cream?" *mmmm*

—*John M. Feierabend*

SONGS

Allee Galloo

Al-lee gal-loo, gal - loo.   Al-lee gal-loo,   gal - lee.

Al   -   lee   gal - loo,   gal-loo,   gal - lee,   WHEEE!

Motions

*Walk around in a circle and kick foot up
high on the word "WHEEE!"
Say the word "WHEEE!" with extreme
vocal inflection.*

Ghost Song

Leader: A wom - an stood at the church - yard door,

Verses & Motions

Group responds to each sung phrase with a ghost sound on "ooooo."

2. And she had not been there before...

3. Oh six long corpses were carried in...

4. So very long and very thin...

5. The woman to the corpses said...

6. "Will I be thus when I am dead?"...

7. The corpses to the woman said *Scream "Ahhhhh."*

Little Red Caboose

Lit-tle red ca-boose,   Lit-tle red ca-boose,

Lit-tle red ca-boose be-hind the train.— Toot, toot,

Smoke stack on its back,   Rol-lin' down the track,

Lit-tle red ca-boose be-hind the train.— Toot, toot.

Motions

*Children follow a leader as he or she weaves
around the room. At the end of the song,
the leader becomes the caboose and the next
in line becomes the new leader. Make sure
the children chant the "toots" in head voice.*

She'll Be Comin' 'Round the Mountain

She'll be com-in' 'round the moun-tain when she comes. *Yee -*

ha! She'll be com-in' 'round the moun-tain when she

comes. *Yee - ha!* She'll be com-in' 'round the

moun-tain, She'll be com-in' 'round the moun-tain, She'll be

com-in' 'round the moun-tain when she comes. *Yee - ha!*

Verse 2

She'll be drivin' six white horses
when she comes...
*Speak "Whoa back" at the end of
phrases 1, 2 and 4.*

Verse 3

Oh, we'll all go down to greet her
when she comes...
*Speak "Hi, ma'am" at the end of
phrases 1, 2 and 4.*

Verse 4

Oh we'll all have chicken and
dumplings when she comes...
*Speak, "Yum, yum" at the end of
phrases 1, 2 and 4.*

BOOKS

Books that lend themselves to pitch exploration sounds:

Georgie the Ghost, by Robert Bright

Ooops! by Suzy Kline

Gingerbread Man, by Paul Galdone

Index